Ocean Soup

A Recipe for You, Me, and a Cleaner Sea

By **MEEG PINCUS** · Illustrated by **LUCY SEMPLE**

From afar the vast ocean appears pure and clean.

How it sparkles and shimmers—a beautiful scene.

But dig in a bit deeper and test a small scoop,
and you'll see that, up close,

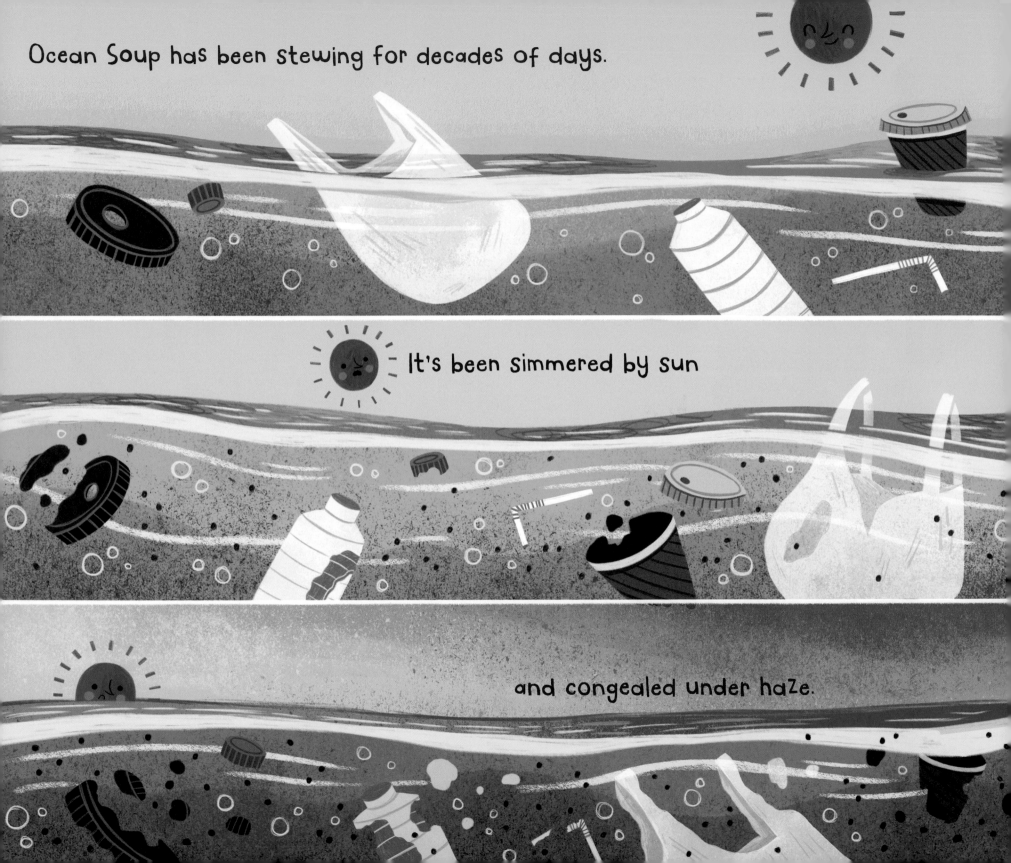

Ocean Soup has been stewing for decades of days.

It's been simmered by sun

and congealed under haze.

Many chefs made this murky, confetti-like brew—
a concoction of habits that bubbled and grew.

It began when a new crop of products first came,
used by folks unaware they'd be later to blame.

They drank coffee from Styrofoam cups topped with lids.

And bought single-use bottles to hydrate their kids.

Out to eat, they grabbed heaps of containers and straws.

And at stores they took throwaway bags without pause.

They used microbead soaps,

wore synthetic attire,

and for parties they blew
up balloons to inspire.

Do you wonder how all this produced Ocean Soup?
How such everyday habits made saltwater goop?

The real problem is plastic; it's in all that stuff.
Whether hard or elastic, that plastic is tough!

Once it's made, any plastic is with us to stay.
It's on Earth till forever—there's no real "away."

People throw out their plastic and think that it's gone,
but most dumps overflow; excess trash just moves on.

Much ends up in the sea,
churning round the five gyres—
the huge saltwater whirlpools
where breakdown transpires.

As time passes,
the gyres turn the plastic to specks,
which then can't be cleaned up,
causing endless effects.

Once the plastic's puréed
in the gyres' mighty waves,
it spills out as a soup
that no animal craves.

Yet it's gulped by the dolphins, the whales, and the seals,

and it's slurped by the fish,

and the plankton

and eels.

It's in icebergs,

in inlets,

the deep ocean floor.

It's snatched up by the seabirds,

the turtles,
and more.

Ocean Soup fills the bellies of all in the sea.
(And if we eat fish too, is it in you and me?)

Are you wishing those chefs had not cooked up this mess?

That they'd known one-use products would cause such distress?

It is time for us new chefs to enter the scene—
with a recipe crafted to get our seas clean.

First, we call on the makers, go straight to the top.
Tell them all of this plastic production must stop!

Then, we practice new habits—preventing more stew—
with reusable items and natural ones, too.

This won't always be easy; we'll all have to think—
to remember our bottles and straws when we drink.

And to carry cloth bags and choose all-cotton clothes.

When we're offered new plastic? Less yesses, more noes!

Ocean Soup may have simmered before we were here,
but the call for us all to pitch in rings out clear.

We will need many chefs to help clean up the sea—
starting here in our kitchen, with you, and with me.

What is Ocean Soup?

Ocean Soup's roots began in the 1940s, when inventors created plastic from leftover waste materials of coal, oil, and gas. In the 1950s, companies touted it as a cheap, light, "throwaway" material and began mass-producing it in many forms. People got used to plastic. Companies today produce nearly 400 million tons of it yearly, less than 10 percent of which is recycled.

This has led to what we call in this book Ocean Soup: the more than 51 trillion particles of "plastic smog" taking over the Earth's oceans. (That's 500 times more plastic particles in the sea than stars in the galaxy!)

It starts with larger plastic pieces that land in the ocean and get sucked into five huge subtropical whirlpools called gyres (rhymes with tires). One, the North Pacific Gyre, is nicknamed The Great Pacific Garbage Patch, which makes it sound like we can see all the trash there and just clean it up—but we can't.

The gyres' circular currents are so strong that a piece of plastic will swirl around for 10 years or more (like a verrrrry long toilet flush!). Amid the currents, waves, and ultraviolet light, plastics in the gyres become brittle and break down into "microparticles" smaller than grains of rice. These seep out into seawater around the globe, creating a toxic "soup" that's impossible to separate.

These are the top four types of plastic that pollute the world's seas—Ocean Soup's main ingredients:

1 Plastic Bags. Americans use 1 million plastic bags *every minute*—only 1 percent of which are recycled.

2 Plastic Bottles. We use 3 million plastic water bottles *every hour*.

4 Styrofoam Cups and Containers. And we use 25 billion Styrofoam coffee cups *every year*—less than 2 percent of which are recycled.

3 Plastic Straws. We use 500 million plastic straws *every day*.

These plastics are the next most common Ocean Soup ingredients:

Microfibers. Some 1.4 trillion "plastic threads" from materials like polyester, nylon, and spandex (think bathing suits, fleece jackets, exercise clothing) have flowed into the ocean, mostly from our home washing machines.

Fishing Gear. Nearly 1.3 billion pounds of plastic fishing lines, nets, and weights also end up in the ocean each year.

Balloons. The amount of plastic balloons and balloon pieces found on beaches has tripled over the past 10 years.

Microbeads. Eight billion tiny plastic balls from toothpastes and soaps have washed down US sinks and showers *each day* for years. (However, thanks to activists, the US and UK recently banned microbead products!)

Remember, none of this plastic will ever fully disintegrate! Our oceans—and all the life-forms in them—are in big trouble. What a mess! So, what can we do about it?!

A Recipe for Cleaner Oceans (in 10 Steps)

We can make a difference! Here's a real-life recipe for how we can reduce
our daily plastic use and help save our world's oceans, wherever we live.

1. Start at the top! Tell companies you want natural, biodegradable, and recycled materials—no more new or single-use plastic! Ask lawmakers to create new laws against producing harmful plastics. (Marine scientists say our best bet to save the oceans is to stop mass plastic production at the source.)

2. Stop and think before you buy stuff. Ask: *do I really need this?* Say no to plastic products and packaging, especially single-use plastic and those top four polluters, whenever you can. Remember: *refuse* comes before reduce, reuse, and recycle!

3. Commit to reusable products. Carry reusable bags, water bottles, straws, and silverware. Reuse containers for food or household cleaners; try bulk refills or DIY recipes.

4. Wear more natural fabrics. Instead of polyester, nylon, and spandex, choose 100% cotton, bamboo, or hemp fabrics. And wash your microfiber clothes infrequently. (You can also add an insert or attachment to your washing machine to catch microfibers.)

5. Use alternatives to balloons for parties or gifts. Try paper streamers, banners or cards, tissue paper pom-poms, or, best yet, real flowers.

6. Pass on fishing. Or, if you must fish, keep your fishing lines and nets from falling into the sea! (You may also want to rethink *eating* fish—scientists are still trying to determine how much of the plastic eaten by fish ends up in the bodies of human fish eaters.)

7. Join cleanups of your local waterways. Whether it's a lake, river, or ocean—it's all connected—there's plastic to be picked up.

8. Find out how to properly recycle or dispose of the plastics you use. Many of us throw unrecyclable or soiled plastics into recycle bins, which can mean the whole batch they're in won't get recycled. Check with your local recycling center for guidelines.

9. Help your communities move toward zero waste. Work with your family, school, city, place of worship, or any local group or business to create zero-waste, plastic-free practices and goals.

10. Keep learning! Check out other books, the 5 Gyres Institute's "Trash Academy" (www.5gyres.org/trash-academy-lessons) and *National Geographic*'s "Kids vs. Plastic" (kids.nationalgeographic.com/explore/nature/kids-vs-plastic).

Just pick *even one step* on this list to start with today. What do you choose?
Every step of this Cleaner Oceans recipe can help!

Author's Note

I grew up, and still live, near the beaches of Southern California, and my favorite childhood memories are of early mornings strolling along the seashore picking up seashells. But the older I've gotten, I'm sad to say, more and more of my beach walking time is spent picking up trash, mostly plastic.

Even worse, it pains me to realize that my own everyday actions are contributing to this huge problem. So, I wrote this book to remind *myself* about my own impact on my beloved ocean, by the daily choices I make, as much as anyone else. We all need to rethink our use of plastic and speak up to manufacturers and lawmakers about its overproduction. It will take a sea change to save our seas—and it starts with each one of us, each day. I commit to doing better. Will you join me?

To Alex Kajitani—amazing surfer, husband, dad, teacher—thanks for your endless support (and for cleaning out the reusable straws!).

—Meeg

For Kristian, for all the support and cups of tea.

—Lucy

Expert Adviser: 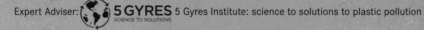 5 Gyres Institute: science to solutions to plastic pollution

SLEEPING BEAR PRESS™

2395 South Huron Parkway, Suite 200
Ann Arbor, MI 48104
www.sleepingbearpress.com

Printed and bound in the United States.

10 9 8 7 6 5 4 3 2
Library of Congress Cataloging-in-Publication Data

Names: Pincus, Meeg, author. | Semple, Lucy, illustrator.
Title: Ocean soup : a recipe for you, me, and a cleaner sea / by Meeg
Pincus ; illustrated by Lucy Semple.
Description: Ann Arbor, Michigan : Sleeping Bear Press, [2021] | Audience:
Ages 6–10 | Summary: "Our oceans are filled with plastics, but who exactly cooked up this soup?
And, more important, what is the recipe for getting our oceans clean? This rhyming story pulls no punches
about how we ended up in this mess but also offers hope and help for cleaning up ocean soup"
– Provided by publisher.
Identifiers: LCCN 2020039824 | ISBN 9781534111189 (hardcover)
Subjects: LCSH: Marine debris—Cleanup—Juvenile literature. | Plastic marine debris—Juvenile literature.
Classification: LCC TD427.M35 P56 2021 | DDC 363.739/4—dc23
LC record available at https://lccn.loc.gov/2020039824

Page 30 Photo Credits: © chones/Adobe.com; © picsfive/Adobe.com; © EuToch/Adobe.com;
© New Africa/Adobe.com; © Noel/Adobe.com; © Eric Dale Creative/Adobe.com